Alba

Caroline Parajo

BookLeaf Publishing

Presentation by *BookLeaf Publishing*

Web: www.bookleafpub.com

E-mail: info@bookleafpub.com

ISBN: 9789357619813

First edition 2022

Paradise

My soul is crying
No silver lining
Chiffon dress on linen
Fell off like my inner demons
It's a fateful evening
Once falling with the season
'Til you flaking your feelings

When I gambled my life
Throwing it by the roll of the dice
In your bed up in skies but instead were out of
our minds

Oh then how, we kept ourselves out of the-
Clothes of clouds, feet let down and set out for -
It's bitter to say, 'there's no other way when the
glimmer dies',

Oh then how we kicked ourselves out of
Paradise
So hope and pray that both someday, no future
dies?

Latched onto gravity
Basked in your mentality

Dewy eyed, next morning
When words of yours left all but brevity
He's gone faithless like her spirit
Her song wasted, dried up lyric
She said 'no higher power or pretty lover will
save me'

Would you spare your entire life
Despair entrance for something out of sight?
Is it better to wait
Is it bitter to taste
Because false hope
Is worse than despair

Oh i'd hate to wait
To tell the truth
When your will is paralysed
When your future fears lies

Yet you roll the dice
Here lies and hopes to land on
Us paragons in a paradigm we call, Paradise

the boy i haven't met irl

sometimes i forget why i even dated you
but you remind me of the days i'm still happy
and breathing
sometimes i forget i even love you,
yeah, you remind me of the odd ways to believe
it
most times i remember to not keep secrets from
you
except to tell you to take some singing lessons
how many kinds of wrapping you think i'll do?
well accept it, it'll keep you guessing
'cause most times i'm the gift that keeps on
giving
and they say keep on counting your blessings
though first impressions count too
oh how grateful i am of having you
yet the blessings i count more,
is how in synchronicity my heart beats with
yours
for every millisecond, there's doors
that open and your song taste starts to crave so
different
how you did a strong play, you pulled me like a
resistance band

a predicament you still haven't met me yet, like
i'm your #1 fan
how well you're shooting your score? a starry
turnout replaced your bedroom blackout
and for our nights are wanderlust and all is well
'til one day us two lovers can meet irl

Love Over Coffee

hi, what can i get for you..
"a cappuccino, thanks,
and to go, please"

...

i'd be your coffee in the morning
craving when you awaken
leave your heart palpitating,
get you sweet-sweet-sweet escaping
i'd be the aroma to your healing
fill that empty, lost feeling
that your heart is deeply missing

is my love not strong enough?
is my love not sweet enough?
just one taste, one single touch

your lips against my mug
from you, is all i ask
addicted to that touch
from that i ask just once,
please, you'll know what you love 'til it's love
over coffee cups

i'd feel the painful memory
your head is always thinking
is remembering
you're always tired of it
so stay in my system of caffeine
'cause you'll fill it with grateful memories
that'll stay deep within

yeah, my love is strong enough
and my love is sweet enough
just a bit o' spice and you'll adjust

your lips against my mug
from you, all i ask
you're addicted to my love
from that i ask just once:
please, you'll know what you love 'til it's love
over coffee cups

i'd be the caffeine boost before your day starts
let you leave a stain on this coffee heart
i'd be your vitamin D from the morning sun
then find the milky way when work is done
i'd be the aroma to your healing as such
like the new car smell that's been bottled up
please bottle up in my coffee, love
please, you'll know what you love 'til it's love
over coffee cups

...
"is that all?"
"make that two, thanks,
and to go, please"

the best things

the best dreams are when you are awake
the best years are when you feel no heartaches
the best art is when it is unfinished
the best start is when you feel ambitious

these are the best things i've listed,
but i'll leave my best wishes
to you

the best clothes are usually worn inside your
own homes
the first and only season are usually the best
shows
the best good food is when your tummy is
turning
the best cool could never really see worse in
friends

the best way to cheer yourself is to cheer
someone else up

yeah the best you, could never really work
when you're after the world

but incase i leave the best for last
i couldn't make an end to my wishes
for you

Seasons

Like the seasons changed
I gave you summers, you gave me fall
I wish I'd never fall, for you
Your heart never really stayed
It turned like the leaves
I wish you'd never leave, so soon

If I could turn back time
I question whether I'd give you
So much space and energy, and time
Why didn't I see the signs
If I knew this weather would turn cool
But we managed to keep our cool, when we said
goodbye

We went through a seasonal phase,
Together we braced when the cold came
And blossomed slowly through the rain
But your heartbeat would freeze,
And my world would then bloom
But to grow apart still hurts
I wouldn't trade the world, for you

Oh I question whether
This dry weather turned cool

What we went through
How we managed to keep our cool
Feels so right to leave,
Feels so right to be free
To fill out life's blanks and thrive without you

seen 11:11

he's a doer
she's a dreamer
to be seen by her
wished to keep her

both eyes wide open, seen 11:11
a numerical haven, miracle saving
her angelic hymn had a nomad staying

to be graced by her presence,
a nuance kept him noticed
she knew once, he saw ones
he made a wish come true that instance

he's expected never
'til the first of October
how does she refuse to leave him
when she'd choose to believe

both eyes wide open, seen 11:11
a numerical haven, miracle saving
her angelic hymn had a nomad staying

to be graced by her presence,
a nuance kept noticed

she knew once, he saw ones
he made a wish come true that instance

Athlete

Love spun petals like a whirlwind
Autumn's got a crush on Spring
Love sunk when you poured a drink
For us

Your skin, scorched by the sun
Could even torch our Love
A smile was more than enough
To float in your head,
For ever

An athlete, you are
Got me running on your mind
Every beat of your heart
Got it placing and claiming first prize
For we're miles apart,
Yet while the sun's gone under,
Smiles got you winning me over

Love's race, peddling on a wheel
Feet told time it was never progressing,
Always, standing still
Love's game, when you played it well

For fun

And Love won, now no war in midst

For miles you'd run on for miles
You'd bet it for a smile

re-ignite

his hands slowly caress my arms
away from the touch screen of his phone
i wrap inside that warm
oven kind of love, feels nice when we're alone

just wait 'til i write you poems and
live to tell each other how we've grown
together, by each other's side, 'til the very end

but i just want my heart to race at the sight of
you
feel me burning infinitely, like all the stars do,
just to say intimately of how much, i-love-you

and you'd tell me funny somethings 'til it makes
me cry
and you'd call me just to say i'm cute sometimes
though i'd spend hours staring, getting lost in
your eyes
yet its not enough,
when we're chasing dying embers
hoping these sparks could
go off
i want that jazzy, soul feeling you could even,
sing to me live

and latin music that keeps you up on your, feet
all night
though i'd spend hours staring, getting lost in
your eyes
yet its not enough,
when we're chasing dying embers
hoping our fading sparks could,
re-ignite

my hands fit into yours perfectly
my head lays onto your chest, just like it came
out of a movie scene we're watching and that
warm fuzzy feeling i get when you speak, just
listening

can't wait 'til you write me poems and
live to tell each other how you've grown
to get me by your side, till the very end

i pray you take me all around the world
i want to be your lover & forever girl
and not leave you at the aisle
hoping our fading sparks could re-ignite,
i wish you don't change
or make me rearrange my things
if you leave
i need you not to be
moving on like a 90s trend
i long for you like the weekend,

but most of all,
i hope our fading sparks could re-ignite

Rollercoaster

I bought a ticket to your mind,
your childish mind
our childish minds
or I bought a ticket to your childish mind
Run wild
While I hide feels of desires
We were mindless bodies, without no thinking
souls
How'd it get out of c-c-control?

I'm hypnotic,
Impulsive,
You got me twisted in your turning
Spiralling, getting sick and dizzy from all of the
Conspiring,
Body heat rising
Only eyes speaking
Only skin flirting
Begging for your loving, touching

Winds whirling,
hands hurling
Telling eyes fell for they locked into mine, I'm
Propelling,
Belted seats fastened

Strapped in your air, gasping
Adrenaline running'
Why give into the rushing

Hair raising, it'd be falling in your face when
We're 30ft floors up, and you fainting,
You question where you put your faith in

We
We're just flying recklessly,
Flight's higher above the scenes
She got him once, he fooled her twice,
Oh shame on me,
but we can blame it on the rollercoaster ride

Fly, thought I took a bad trip up your sky,
Pleading off this guilty high,
Leading back to the thoughts of us,
Rush dives
Into a world of mine
You can forgive your body, but your mind don't
forget
How can you let it g-g-go?

Yeah I loved the part, you get me into the
d-d-dark
Music box winding, your world aloft
Hanging onto dear life, 'til death to us part
Yeah you got me riding on then riding off

A clouded attraction beneath your highness
Is this seat taken?
To fill this attraction
I contain constellations in my mind
and all of my stars dance for you

blue

did you ever wanna swing by mine,
I'm forever in your safe side
how my mind's a'craze
it's all too easy to run, run away,
you never left but a fight to go by
I was never late for catching my ride,
too easy to stay
we'd wait for the next, next train

we've been sitting on this platform for more than
a 'how's your day' exchange
living backwards, i'm taken to 'ol days of what
is now not the same,
how we've now both changed

now my light is changing colours off the sky
up with kisses that would fly and gifted down
onto you
I miss this, and how we talked through the night
be wishing this trust was fully fixed like it used
too,
been seeing that my cup is half empty, and you
see your's half full,
but pieces of my heart broken into two

do you go by the rules,
how I played off field,
or caught you off guard
do you watch by the pool
swim a tug of war feels
i could help to win your heart,

but why am I so blue
maybe, I was made to bloom?
when you can't work out things, do they even
work for you?
where can I lay the wounds,
baby I need to know soon,
what had let you down
'cause my view now
is an altered blue
my sky's an altered blue
is it even for you?
i'm still all for you

without 'years of experience' on lonesome terms
how is it that days, weeks, months have been
adjourned
and do you still keep that guitar pick i gave to
you, the 'specially engraved one

i'm even more sadder, you're bluer
and maybe I'll be a late bloomer

how things can't work out now but to pray they
do for you
you were laying out wounds,
take a break to untold news
what had let me down is that my view
since, the sky's an altered blue
is it even for you?
still i'm oddly here for you

it's so severed, so cut off
we spoke about our futures and our roughs,
old feuds and sweet endeavours
is it mean that I'm not there more than enough?
If I hold back my tongue
my thumb says either way
I could scroll just to cling on
The feed show would run thoughts
But to wait would be a waste one would say
'only one would say'
hopefully that ain't you

Beautiful Mosaic

Memories are made,
But the worst thing is that your smile and laugh
will remain
I'll be your view babe,
Caught you looking for a while
I made you stop and stay

But it'll only take a second
For me to be a wreck and
Im asking myself when will the pain end,
Seeing and meeting new faces
Filling my empty spaces
Hoping one day I'll stand again,
But by then,

I'll be a beautiful mosaic
Shining like the stars
Every night and day
I'll be a beautiful mosaic
All my glass-like scars
Have ached me to say
Yes I am a beautiful mosaic
Beautiful beautiful mosaic

Memories only to break
I was in pieces, but you gave me peace
Conversations were made
And you recognised all the cracks in me

It'll only take a second
For me to be a wreck and
Im asking myself when will the pain end
I'll be on display
For more than one last day
I hope I won't be a youthful mistake
Yet instead,

I'll be a beautiful mosaic
Shining like the stars
Every night and day
I'll be a beautiful mosaic
All my glass-like scars
Have ached me to say
Yes I am a beautiful mosaic
Beautiful, beautiful mosaic

All my broken then turning beautiful
Hurts to notice, when feelings mutual
Once been broken, now turning beautiful
All so potent when healings are wonderfully
made
Yeah, my smile and laugh will remain

wishful forecast

don't really need to be forward,
i feel like we're going backwards

just to be honest
and that's a promise

i'm no forecaster
but i see a future with you

Fickle in Fools

We ate forbidden fruit
We broke all the rules
Led to dangerous routes
Left our fingerprints as clues
That's the fickle in fools

Changing minds like the season,
Switching sides, got one foot out, other one in
The new door that got us placing old keys in

We're back to the beginning,
How did I end up with you?
Rekindling the flame once again

I'm kind enough not to blame
Don't want it to burn you this time,
Survive what still remains
Let's do the crashing, burning, rushing and
yearning again,
Everlast in the aftermath
It's debri in Spring

How you got wrecked, I was in ruin
Cigars and liquor were your friends
Mine was mind, paper and pen

Time was awfully spent
To write for fickle in fools
Hope it was fulfilling for you

Changing waters, cutting stems,
Window wipers, windows down, let the water in
The new car that got us placing old keys in

love potion

no we don't need no history
so skip the movie edits
we'll roll our own credits
and make our own comments
'cause that's the way you live it
young girls tend to dream it
before they could hear the curtains closing

hope we got this chemistry
'cause you were playing games then,
the kind that bad boys tend,
tend to be good at to win
now you quit and it seems I bit
the substance that turns a love potion
and the touch that becomes to close in

Fallen Angel

Touchdown, Top Gun good lookin'
Fine lines so divine
I see the end more than this beginning
See through my flask of pink wine
You start sweet talkin'
Remind me why I was f
                    a
                  l
                    l
                  i
                n
              g and staring?
Eye stopping, glaring gives me the adrenaline
Jaw dropping, got me in my tracks stopping,
Boy did you f
              a
              l
              l

              i
              n
            from the sky?
A breathless sight
A perfect strike
And heaven will know my sin

But it sent me this kind of blessing, well
Think I was compelled to the ways
You might of f
                e
            l
             l
From hell, I'd think again
Baby you're saved by grace when
My heart pieced into place and everything
        f
      e
      l
   l for your chasing embrace
Oh how I trust-fall for the danger
Of falling in love with a fallen angel

wet pillow

You're falling hard in love for me
You can't keep me, but only the memory
It's tougher to be sober once you drink
romanticised wine
When you served me a platter of butterflies
It was nauseous and cautious of me to think
otherwise
To silence my body that filled you with answers
To dampen the pillow rather than cry in prayers
Falling out of love is hard, you see
You're just a loner wandering through life
While I'm a lover who tried

Skydiving

Stars picket fence the sky
For a hand-written mail in boxes to find
Handsome prince felt in need to fly
Encouraged him not to pick this plight
Instead he jumped off a plane...

He hung by clouds that hear the cursing,
He's familiar with the down, 'cause he'd know
what's worse than
Visiting other places in and out of town, as time
goes all too freely
He'd say 'It's only fallin' baby,
not more than once, but frequently'

See I'd take you and your hand
Like I care, but you can't dance
You'd be free for find me
Fighting the adrenaline I'd breathe,
A hundred times over
See I'd do it, i'd countdown from three
But to jump a hundred times over
That's you, not me

Darling angel picked off a page
Handing a mark that fails to say
your name
Encouraged him not to stay awake
Encouraged him not to wait
Instead he jumped off a plane...

You'd collect my only words,
And from one, I'd be gone instead
On my fingertips up against
The mind I'm settling
Eyes are widening the sky
My baby hanging from a cloud

without me, you'd hear the cursing,
You're familiar with the sound,
'cause you know what's worse than
Hearing a voice quite so loud
Always as time goes all too quickly
I'd say 'It's nearly fallin' but more than usually"

I could wish on a star,
For you to be loved
First
Touch
And the world and our cares go far
Longing for a tight hold
I could drown in your love but
First

Jump
You'd already go-

Skydiving from the moon
Sailing on an ocean so blue
Hear the parachute pulled
Pray the winds are helping you,
For the landing to stay
The motions all too soon, you'll blame
Wind in ear screams 'woo' instead you wave
'Bye' to that angel still up at the plane

paint me, love

panning across moonscape, you be lightyears
away
stars can align for some days but out of all days,
you would be - the mineral, the gem spot off the
sea
you're in every corner of my mind that wants to
plead,
to turn every song into smiles
every picture, memorised
can't do work when staring at a blank canvas
feel the rain waiting by stemmed roses, the
chances of
infinite petals are too true
and in français, they say:
"la vie est belle, l'amour toujours"
which means:
"life is beautiful, always love it"

Ingram Content Group UK Ltd.
Milton Keynes UK
UKHW021828250723
425770UK00016B/738